The Rockwool Foundation Research Unit

The Effect of Workfare on Crime:
Youth Diligence and Law Obedience

Peter Fallesen, Lars Pico Geerdsen,
Susumu Imai, and Torben Trænæs

University Press of Southern Denmark
Odense 2012

The Effect of Workfare on Crime:
Youth Diligence and Law Obedience

Study Paper No. 41

Published by:
© The Rockwool Foundation Research Unit and
University Press of Southern Denmark

Copying from this book is permitted only within
institutions that have agreements with CopyDan,
and only in accordance with the limitations laid
down in the agreement

Address:
The Rockwool Foundation Research Unit
Sølvgade 10
DK-1307 Copenhagen K

Telephone   +45 33 34 48 00

Fax   +45 33 34 48 99

E-mail   forskningsenheden@rff.dk

Home page   www.rff.dk

ISBN 978-87-90199-66-1
ISSN 0908-3979
January 2012
Print run: 300
Printed by   Specialtrykkeriet Viborg A/S

Price: 60.00 DKK, including 25% VAT

Contents

Abstract	5
1 Introduction	7
2 Labor Market Programs in Denmark and Farum	11
3 Data	14
4 Empirical Model	22
5 Estimation Results	27
6 Concluding Remarks	42
References	43
A Appendix	46

The Effect of Workfare on Crime: Youth Diligence and Law Obedience [*]

Peter Fallesen, Rockwool Foundation
Lars Pico Geerdsen, Krak's Foundation
Susumu Imai, Queen's University
and Torben Tranæs, Rockwool Foundation[†]

Abstract

In this paper, we estimate the effect of workfare policy on crime by exploiting two exogenous welfare policy changes in Denmark. Our results show a strong decline in the crime rate among treated unemployment uninsured men relative to untreated uninsured and unemployment insured men, and part of this decline can be identified as a direct effect of workfare participation. Moreover, we find that criminal activity was also reduced during weekends, when the workfare programs were closed, which suggests a change in attitude among the participants. These results imply a strong and potentially lasting crime reducing effect of workfare policy.

Keywords: crime reduction, difference-in-differences, policy experiment, secondary effects, workfare policy

---

[*]The authors thank Lance Lochner, Steve Machin, Panu Poutvaara, Francis Kramarz, Christian Dustman, Torbjørn Skardhammar, Elisabeth Savage, Florence Goffet-Nagot, Britta Kyvsgaard, and Anne-Marie Heckscher for helpful comments on earlier versions. We also thank conference and seminar participants at Hitotsubashi University, University of Technology Sydney, City University London, GATE Lyon, CESifo, EALE, EEA, ESC, Stockholm Criminology Symposium, and University of Vienna. This work was funded by the Rockwool Foundation. Responsibility lies solely with the authors.

[†]Corresponding author. Rockwool Foundation Research Unit, Sølvgade 10, 2. tv., DK-1307 Copenhagen K. Web: www.rff.dk Email: tt@rff.dk.

1 Introduction

For centuries, inactivity has been blamed for antisocial and self-destructive behaviors like crime and alcoholism. This notion dates back at least to the early modern era, with its poorhouses and forced labor, where people were not allowed to simply wander about without means of support. These impoverished people were rounded up and detained in correction facilities, had they not already admitted themselves to a workhouse of similar sort. The argument for this practice was not just the prevention of the crime that their lack of income might trigger. Another important argument for keeping people occupied was that it made it possible to train them in the received social norms (Foucault, 1975). In modern days we have seen the same line of reasoning used in relation to workfare and increasingly so over the last two decades. Several arguments have been put forward for not giving poor people pecuniary benefits unconditionally. Work-in-return schemes will prevent the not-so-needy from claiming benefits if the work requirement is high enough (Besley and Coate, 1992, 1995); also, authorities argue that being active is good for the needy themselves (Torfing, 1999). It keeps the needy alert, helps them maintain their skills and qualities, trains their social skills, reduces the temptation to engage in high-risk behavior, etc.

In this paper we study the effect of inactivity on crime. More specifically, we study the effect of workfare or active labor market programs on participants' criminal activities. We intent to isolate the effect of 'being active' by comparing the behavior of groups of individuals who are treated differently if they experience unemployment; those who receive only pecuniary benefits (welfare) with those who are also enrolled in mandatory activation (workfare).

In many countries there has been a high level of interest in applying active labor market policies (ALMPs),[1] i.e., work or training requirements, to jobless individuals who receive unemployment insurance or welfare payments, as a way of helping these people into employment. The fact that these programs continue even though the employment effect of the active policies is mixed at best (see Heckman et al., 1999) suggests that the programs may have a broader purpose than simply increasing employment; e.g., poverty alleviation as discussed in Besley and Coate (1995) or improvements of UI schemes as analyzed in Kreiner and Tranæs (2005). Participation in the programs may also help individuals to abstain from criminal activity.[2] In fact, the social benefit obtained from crime reduction

---

[1] From now on, we will use the terms *mandatory work and training requirement*, *mandatory work requirement*, *workfare*, *activation policy*, *active labor market policy*, and *active labour market programs* interchangeably, with the same meaning.

[2] This also links to the literature on unemployment and crime. The existence of a strong positive relationship between unemployment and crime has been hypothesized for almost a hundred years in the social sciences literature (see Cantor and Land (1985) for details). Reviews of the literature can be found

can be greater than the benefit obtained from the reduction in welfare dependency. Crime imposes strong negative externality on the community, and the conventional methods for reducing crimes, such as incarceration, may be much more costly than workfare policies.[3]

The issue is relevant not just for those European countries where ALMPs are applied to unemployed workers on UI benefits or welfare, but also for countries such as the U.S. that have high crime rates. Much research has been done on what government and local communities can do to reduce crime rate in the U.S. Donohue III and Siegelman (1998) survey studies of whether U.S. social programs reduce crime.[4] They discuss the Job Corps program at length, because they argue that it has the most promise in terms of reduction in crime.[5] The program is estimated to reduce overall crime by 12%. Note that in most of those programs, participants not only self-select into the program but are also carefully screened. In contrast, the ALMPs are most often applied to anybody whose enrollment on welfare has exceeded the passive period.

Participation in an ALMP may influence the risk of individuals committing crime in various ways. First, ALMPs may reduce crime among welfare recipients indirectly through an increase in employment; either because of higher income or because of more hours being actively occupied. Since the employment effect of ALMPs is, at best, small on average, its effect on crime through this channel is expected to be small as well. Second, ALMPs might impact crime indirectly though an increase in income if program participants receive higher benefits than other unemployed people.

Third, the active programs may have a direct effect because work, training or education may simply leave less time for crime. According to Jacob and Lefgren (2003), when students are given days off from school exogenously, they commit more property crimes and fewer violent crimes. Jacob and Lefgren measure the intensive margin of the effect of schooling on crime of students who attend classes regularly. Those who would be the most at risk of committing crimes may also rarely come to school, and thus may only be

---

in Wilson (1983), Long and Witte (1981), and Chiricos (1987). According to Chiricos (1987) and Levitt (2001), there is a predominance of estimates showing a positive correlation between unemployment and property crime. For unemployment and violent crimes, however, the connection does not seem to be equally clear.

[3]The cost of incarceration not only includes the direct cost of the criminal justice system, but also dynamic costs, which are the stigma of an arrest record and criminal human capital accumulation in prison. Bayer et al. (2009) forcefully argue that prison environments greatly facilitate criminal human capital accumulation through learning from the peers.

[4]Lochner (2011) also extensively surveys the studies of the crime reduction effects of education and job training programs.

[5]Job Corps is a residential program where economically-disadvantaged youths aged 16 to 21 voluntarily participate in educational and training programs for seven months. In order to stay in the program, participants must not be arrested for felonies, must pass drug tests, must avoid fighting, and must not commit robbery or sexual assault. They must also abide by other rules, such as rules on dress and appearance, as well as dormitory inspection rules.

weakly affected by the policy. Fourth, in the case of ALMPs the extensive margin could also be important. That is, workfare programs may change the lifestyle of the welfare recipients from one that is susceptible to criminal activity to one that is not: for instance, to one that is driven by the expectation of a better future, a future which a criminal record could jeopardize.

To test these hypotheses, we study the workfare policy in Denmark, focusing on the effect for unemployed uninsured welfare recipients; a group with a high crime rate and a group to whom the employment effect has been particularly weak.[6] The dataset we have allows us to separately estimate each of the aforementioned effects of workfare. First, since we have data on whether individuals are working in regular jobs or in workfare programs, we can separate the indirect effect through subsequent employment from the direct effects of activation. Second, the information on individual income allows us to separately control for changes in income associated with workfare program participation. Finally, to separately identify the intensive and extensive marginal effects, we use an unconventional source of information: from 1991 we have information on the exact dates of crimes committed. We separate the crimes between those committed on weekdays, when unemployed individuals on workfare are engaged in training or public relief jobs, and the crimes committed at weekends, when those programs are closed.

Estimating the causal effect of program participation poses a challenge because many unobserved characteristics or events that make individuals more likely to participate in a certain program also make them more likely to commit crime.[7] We address the endogeneity issue of program participation by exploiting two types of policy change. First, we analyze the effect of a radical workfare reform in a municipality. In 1987, Farum, a Danish municipality, introduced an immediate ALMP participation requirement for all

---

[6]Both Bolvig et al. (2003) and Graversen (2004) find that most training programs have a large lock-in effect, which reduces the transition out of unemployment during the program period, but that the programs only have modest treatment effects after the program-period. Bolvig et al. (2003) find negligible lock-in effects and strong treatment effect for both private and public employment programs, whereas Graversen (2004) finds the treatment effect only for the private employment programs. But Graversen also finds that private employment programs are more effective with workers who have characteristics that make them more employable than the other welfare recipients.

[7]This is parallel to the challenge when studying the effect of unemployment on crime. Here, researchers have tried to find exogenous variations that affect unemployment but do not affect crime directly. Raphael and Winter-Ebmer (2001) use closing of military bases and Gould et al. (2002) and Fougére et al. (2009) use changes in industry structure as the exogenous variation. Note that plant closing or changes in industry structure could affect local communities directly, or it could lead to changes in their anti-crime policies, and thus change the crime rate. Oster and Agell (2007) estimate the effect of unemployment and labor market program participation on crime using Swedish municipality-level data, where they use lagged unemployment and lagged labor market program participation as instruments. Recently, some literature has addressed the relationship between welfare benefits and crime using regional level data. Machin and Marie (2006) study the effect of the tightening of unemployment benefit rules on the crime rate and find a positive causal relationship. They use the predicted fraction of individuals that would be adversely affected by the tougher unemployment benefit standards as the instrument.

individuals who received welfare benefits, i.e., unemployed individuals without unemployment insurance (no-UI). In the rest of Denmark, ALMP participation would normally not occur until individuals had received welfare benefits continuously for at least three months and usually much longer. We use the introduction of immediate activation in Farum as treatment and examine its causal effect on crime in Farum compared to the rest of Denmark.

Second, we examine the effects of a series of national reforms of activation policy for young welfare recipients that were introduced during the 1990s, and the municipality level variation in the enforcement of these reforms. These reforms strengthened the work requirement; they were introduced gradually, being applied first to the youngest welfare participants. We exploit both the differential introduction of the workfare reforms across different age groups and the municipality-level differences in its actual enforcement.

Both in Farum and at the national level, ALMPs are estimated to have had a statistically and economically significant negative effect on crime for the no-UI individuals, but to have had no effect or a positive one for UI individuals. Furthermore, the effect is significant even if we control for welfare participation. Thus, we argue that an important source of the policy effect comes from the direct effect of activation on those who stay on welfare. Also, the policy is estimated to have reduced both weekday crimes and weekend crimes. Hence, it seems that at least some of the reduction in crime is due to a positive change in lifestyles, and not only to the reduction in leisure hours. This suggests that the effect could be long-lasting.

In Section 2, we explain the institutional details of the welfare and workfare policies in Denmark, the national-level workfare reforms of the 1990s, and the unique welfare policy experiment in the Danish municipality of Farum. In Section 3, we discuss the details of the panel data we assembled from the Danish register. In Section 4, we present the empirical model and the estimation strategy. In Section 5 we report the estimation results, and in Section 6 we conclude.

2 Labor Market Programs in Denmark and Farum

2.1 Unemployment Benefits and Welfare in Denmark

In Denmark, unemployed individuals fall into two categories: those who are members of an unemployment insurance fund (UI fund), which is a voluntary system in Denmark (see Parsons et al., 2003) and those who are not. The former are entitled to UI benefits and the latter to means-tested welfare benefits. Hence, individuals with personal savings or an employed spouse may not be entitled to any assistance, or may be subject to some reduction in the amount unless they are UI fund members. At the beginning of the 1990s an individual had to be working for an employer, be self-employed, or to have participated in an recognized course of post-secondary education of at least 18 months duration to qualify for membership of the UI fund.

Individuals eligible for welfare are younger, are less highly educated, have less work experience and have had longer unemployment periods compared to individuals eligible for UI. Welfare eligible individuals also tend to be less integrated in society, more likely to indulge in alcohol or drug abuse, and suffer physical or mental health problems. Furthermore, relatively large fractions of the welfare benefit recipients in Denmark are composed of immigrants and refugees. More than two thirds of immigrants and refugees are not included in the official unemployment statistics, since they are not considered to be immediately available for work (Graversen, 2004).

Both UI and welfare are administered locally, through the local UI fund and the local municipalities, respectively. For the UI benefits, the local UI fund has to follow the national policy strictly. For welfare benefits, municipalities are allowed to deviate substantially from the national policy, or at least, deviations are tolerated. During the 1990s, several changes were made to the welfare system. More and more emphasis was put on workfare (activation), especially for the young.

In July 1990 the youth-benefit law ("Ungdomsydelse") was introduced. Originally, it only applied to individuals below the age of 20, but in October 1991 it was extended to cover 20-year-olds. The law stated that in order to receive welfare benefits, the unemployed person had to register. Then, within 2 weeks of registration, s/he could expect to receive a mandatory activation offer. That is, s/he would be given either government subsidized private employment, public relief work, or a place on a training program, all to start immediately on the receipt of the notification. The activation requirement lasted for at least 5 months; this period was extended to 8 months in 1992, but the law still only applied to people up to and including the age of 20.

In 1994, the law was amended so that individuals below age 25 and receiving welfare were to start mandatory activation after no more than 13 weeks of unemployment, and those older than 25 after no more than 12 months of unemployment (Brogaard and Weisse, 1997). Since 1995, the activation requirements for welfare recipients have been gradually strengthened. In 1995 the mandatory weekly hours of activation were increased from 20 hours to 30 hours. In 1996 the mandatory activation period was extended from 6 months to 18 months, and in January 1998 the activation requirement was strengthened again to cover all individuals below the age 30 after 13 weeks of unemployment.

The actual implementation of the ALMPs for the unemployed no-UI workers was left to the local municipalities, and many of them delayed the activation programs or reduced them, due to lack of resources. Some municipalities implemented more ambitious activation schemes that started earlier and were more intensive than laid down in the national guidelines. Hence, there existed a substantial heterogeneity in implementation at the municipality level.

Mandatory activation was also introduced as part of the UI scheme during the 1990s. However, the introduction came later for UI indiciduals and never approached immediate activation. At the end of the 1990s the passive period for unemployed UI workers was a full year. Thus, the treatment was much weaker for UI individuals, who also commit far less crime.

2.2 The case of Farum

During the 1980s the Danish municipalities sent individuals receiving welfare payments into activation only after a very long period of unemployment, and only if the municipality believed that the individuals were not capable of finding work themselves. The activation programs in Farum were similar in character until the end of 1986 and focused on employment/activation in service jobs within the municipality, such as shoveling snow for the elderly, cleaning up local nature reserves, etc. (Birkbak, 1997, p. 13).

In 1986, the municipality of Farum appointed Lars Bjerregård as its employment consultant.[8] Shortly thereafter, in May 1987, the municipality started to make a series of radical changes to its activation policy for recipients of welfare (unemployed no-UI individuals).

First, the no-UI unemployed workers were activated on the very first day they applied for welfare. Second, the activated individuals were mainly sent to work in private firms. If it was not possible to find a suitable position in a private firm, from May 1987 the individual concerned was assigned to work at the local activation facility called "Production House".

---

[8]He was appointed head of the employment administration in 1991.

Farum introduced the policy changes over the period from late 1986 through 1990. From 1988 individuals with physical or mental disabilities who received welfare benefits were also subject to lighter forms of activation. People such as alcoholics and drug addicts were sent for mandatory treatment. From 1990, *all* uninsured welfare recipients were subject to immediate activation. Farum made no distinctions based on age-groups, gender, education or any demographic characteristic (other than mental or physical disabilities) (Birkbak, 1997).

In late 1990s and early 2000s, Farum relaxed their activation policies in response to a series of lawsuits from Danish labor unions and complaints from the Ministry of Employment alleging that these policies violated the laws protecting workers and gave unfair competitive advantages to some firms.[9] Even though the activation experiment in Farum had been heavily criticized, the Danish national government effectively adopted it, so that by 1998 welfare recipients below the age of 30 were placed in mandatory activation schemes very similar to that of Farum. Later reforms in 2002 further increased the similarities. The difference was that the implementation of the national policy was still weaker than the one of Farum.

---

[9] In particular, there were allegations made by labor unions in 2000-2001 that some firms were given favorable access to activated workers as cheap labor and were able to make contracts with the Production House. In 2000, the Danish parliament started to discuss the matter. In 2002, after a series of newspaper reports on the allegations, the Minister of Employment asked Mayor Brixtofte of Farum to adjust the workfare programs to address those concerns. Then the Anti-Trust Board of Denmark formally launched an investigation into the anticompetitive nature of the program. Several years later, the activation operation at the Production House was found to be illegal and it was closed in 2006.

3 Data

3.1 Danish Register Data

In Denmark, every person is given a unique personal code called a CPR-number (Central Personal Register number) at birth or immigration. This code is used every time a person is in contact with a public authority. Information on the person obtained by the government is saved at Statistics Denmark. All individuals are tracked until they either die or emigrate. The result is an extremely detailed panel data set for the entire Danish population extending over more than 25 years that has information on demographic, educational, income, and labor market outcomes. From the police departments we also have information on each individual's criminal record.

Our focus will be on men between the ages of 18 and 30 (35 in case of the national reforms), who have by far the highest crime rate compared to any other demographic groups. Approximately 25% of all Danish men have been arrested before the age of 30 (Tranæs and Geerdsen, 2008). At the same time, this specific age group has been the target of numerous labor market reforms since the late 1980s.

3.2 Crime measures

Our measure of criminal activity is the number of arrests that led to a guilty verdict in court. From now we will simply call it arrests. We also call the average number of arrests for a group simply the arrest rate for the group. We use the date when the crime was committed as the date corresponding to an arrest.

We obtain information on criminal activity from the Central Crime Register. It provides data on all arrests recorded by the Danish police. The data consist of all charges filed against individuals, both primary or secondary. The information includes whether the case went to court and the subsequent verdict, including whether the charges were withdrawn or not, and whether the case was dismissed in court or not. It also has information on incarcerations: type and place of prison, and actual time spent in jail.

The register covers the period 1981 to 2005. Information in the register can be merged with all the other information that we have access to through the perpetrators' CPR numbers.[10]

---

[10]Danish Criminal Register does not have information on date of crime committed before 1990 and the ones recorded in 1990 may not be very accurate. To deal with this issue, we impute the crime date for the crimes committed before 1991 based on the difference in crime date and arrest date observed after 1991.

3.3 Descriptive statistics for Farum and the rest of Denmark

In Table 1 we present some sample statistics of the variables used in our analysis. The sample consists of all men between the ages 18 and 30 in the municipality of Farum, and the corresponding 5% random sample drawn from the rest of Denmark. The data are from the period 1981 to 2005. We find that in Farum fewer young men were insured against unemployment than in the rest of Denmark. We also find that they had a somewhat higher arrest rate and slightly lower level of education than those in the rest of Denmark. The more pronounced difference between Farum and the rest of Denmark was in the marriage rate. Young men in Farum were more likely to be married and have children, which could be related to the fact that a higher proportion of young men in Farum were immigrants from non-Western countries.[11]

Next, we compare the sample statistics of the UI and no-UI men. We first note that the arrest rate for the no-UI men is more than twice as high as that for the UI men, both in Farum and in the rest of Denmark. The arrest rate for insured individuals is also higher in Farum than in the rest of Denmark, but it is lower in Farum for the no-UI individuals. This difference could be mainly due to the fact that during the sample period, the no-UI individuals in Farum were subject to a very strict activation policy, which we argue reduced their criminal activities. Furthermore, the UI men were on average older and more highly educated than the no-UI individuals. In Farum, the unemployment insured were twice as likely to be married as the no-UI group, and in the rest of Denmark, they were 60% more likely to be married.

In the rest of Denmark, the proportion of the population made up of native Danes and immigrants from Western countries was larger for the unemployment insured than for the uninsured, but interestingly, the opposite was the case in Farum. In Farum the no-UI men were twice as likely be living with their parents as the insured. In the rest of Denmark, the unemployment uninsured were more likely to stay with parents than the UI individuals, but the difference is not as large as in Farum. Lastly, in Farum the uninsured were much more likely to live in the same municipality as their parents than the insured, but in the rest of Denmark, the insured had a slightly higher probability of doing so than the uninsured. These differences could also explain the difference in arrest rates between Farum and the rest of Denmark for the no-UI and UI groups. For the descriptive statistics for the national sample, see Table 12 in the Appendix.

Next, we look at the time series plots of several key national level variables to see the effect of a series of activation reforms that were implemented at the national level during

---

[11]We decided to use immigrants from Western countries instead of those from developed countries because during the period of 1981 to 2003, many countries grew out of the developing country status. In any case, the difference between the two classifications is very minor.

Table 1: Sample Statistics

Variable	Total				no-UI				UI			
	Farum		Denmark		Farum		Denmark		Farum		Denmark	
	mean	sd	mean	sd	mean	sd	mean	sd	mean	sd	mean	sd
Unemployment Insured	0.531	0.499	0.644	0.479								
Arrest Rate	0.068	0.342	0.062	0.327	0.097	0.410	0.106	0.444	0.042	0.266	0.037	0.236
Age	24.80	3.576	25.20	3.417	23.57	3.688	23.99	3.754	25.89	3.088	25.87	3.013
Years of Schooling	10.75	2.495	10.90	2.273	10.30	2.274	10.29	2.257	11.16	2.611	11.23	2.212
Higher Education	0.416	0.493	0.476	0.499	0.243	0.429	0.261	0.439	0.570	0.495	0.596	0.491
Married	0.229	0.420	0.173	0.378	0.136	0.343	0.121	0.327	0.310	0.463	0.201	0.401
Having children	0.237	0.425	0.211	0.408	0.166	0.372	0.156	0.363	0.300	0.458	0.242	0.428
Western or Danish	0.838	0.369	0.946	0.225	0.871	0.335	0.924	0.265	0.808	0.394	0.959	0.199
Parents, same home	0.311	0.463	0.200	0.400	0.423	0.494	0.257	0.437	0.222	0.416	0.171	0.377
Parents, same municipality	0.511	0.500	0.483	0.500	0.601	0.490	0.462	0.499	0.440	0.496	0.494	0.500
Sample Size	273,007		1,884,703		128,100		671,301		144,907		1,213,402	

Source: Own calculations on data from Statistics Denmark

Data

Figure 1: Arrest Rate of no-UI Men, 1981-2005

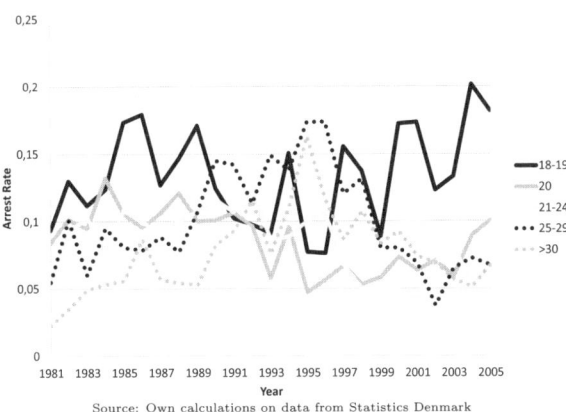

Source: Own calculations on data from Statistics Denmark

the 1990s. If we look at Figure 1 where we plot the arrest rates of no-UI men in different age groups, we clearly see the effects of the three main activation reforms for no-UI workers implemented over the 1990s. The arrest rate of 18- to 19-year-old men decreased in 1990. The arrest rate of 20-year-olds declined sharply after 1992. For the individuals aged 21 to 24, arrest rates declined sharply after 1992 and again after 1996, which was two years after the activation rule was gradually strengthened through a sequences of reforms. Finally, the arrest rate for the age 25 to 29 years group dramatically decreased in 1998, when the welfare reforms were applied to them. A caveat to be mentioned though is that the decline in the arrest rate often seems to occur a bit later than the years when the reform was enacted. In our opinion, this reflects the lags at the municipality level in enforcing the policy; a point we shall return to later.

On the other hand, it is worth mentioning that the time series pattern for the arrest rates for UI men of different age groups does not follow the pattern we just saw, i.e., is not related to the timing of the activation reforms for the no-UI men; see Figure 7 in the Appendix.

A straight forward explanation for a possible effect of the activation reforms on the arrest rates would be that the mandatory activation policies have been very effective in getting young people off the dole and into either employment or ordinary education. Looking at the Danish National unemployment rates for no-UI men of different ages, Figure 2, gives exactly this impression. In particular for the three youngest groups, the period when unemployment rate started to go down roughly coincided with the period when the mandatory activation was introduced for the groups concerned. However, looking at the unemployment rate may be misleading in this regard, because while the unemployment is

Figure 2: Unemployment Rate, no-UI and UI Men age 18 to 30 years, 1981-2005

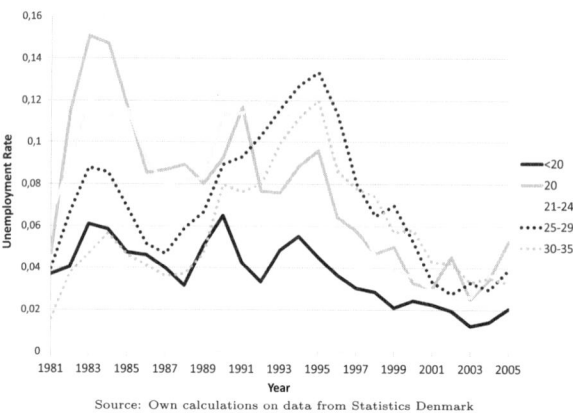

Figure 3: Fraction of men at School or Regular Job, 1981-2005

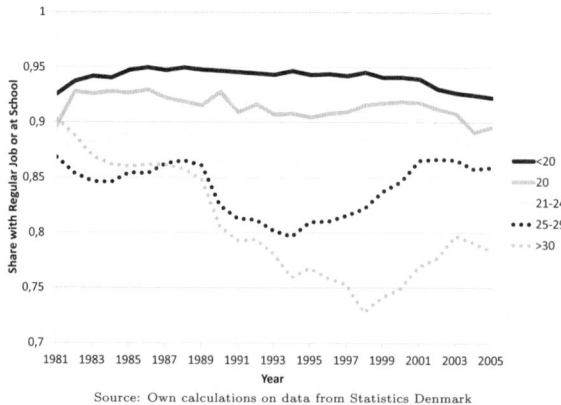

Figure 4: Unemployment Rate, no-UI and UI Men age 18 to 30 years, 1981-2005

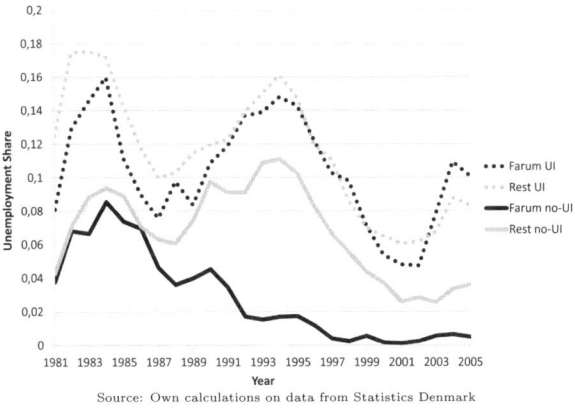

Source: Own calculations on data from Statistics Denmark

a category that includes people who are on welfare and look for jobs, it does not include individuals who are in activation programs. That is, the decline in unemployment mainly reflects an increase in the participation in active programs like public sector relief job, subsidized private sector training, etc., and not an increase in employment or ordinary education. In fact the reforms did not seem to have caused a major shift of people into employment or ordinary education. Figure 3 plots the proportions of men in schooling or regular jobs for different age groups. The years with the lowest levels of men in schooling or regular jobs for each age group do not coincide with the years of the activation policy reform, and there is either a declining trend or no trend at all over the reform period as a whole. This illustrates the points from the recent literature that evaluates the active labor market policies in Denmark, such as Bolvig et al. (2003) and Graversen (2004), namely that ALMPs don't appear to have a substantial employment effect.

Next, we present time series plots of various statistics for Farum and the rest of Denmark. In Figure 4, we plot the average unemployment rate for uninsured and insured men in Farum and the rest of Denmark. Until 1986, they were very similar. However, after 1987, when the activation reform was introduced in Farum, the unemployment rate for no-UI men in Farum continued to decline, whereas that for the rest of Denmark increased sharply up until 1995. From 1995 onward, unemployment rates of no-UI men in both Farum and the rest of Denmark declined over time. This was mainly due to the effects of the implementation of the active labor market policies nationwide. After around 2000, the gap in unemployment rates between Farum and the rest of Denmark was much smaller than before. This corresponds to the time when the activation policies of Farum and the rest of Denmark converged.

Figure 5: Arrest Rate, no-UI Men, 1981-2005

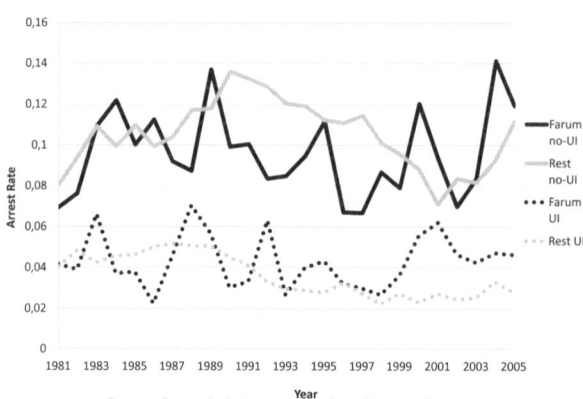

Source: Own calculations on data from Statistics Denmark

In 2002, the national activation policy became almost the same as the one in Farum, except for stricter implementation in Farum. The unemployment rate for no-UI individuals in Farum was still exceptionally low even after 2002, the year when the Farum activation policy started to unravel. This is because the unemployment statistics do not include those on welfare who are deemed not employable. During the periods of very low aggregated unemployment rate for the no-UI men, the variations in the unemployment rate were primarily due to the differences in who among the welfare recipients the municipality would classify as employable. The national activation reforms targeting the unemployable only started much later, around 2004. The unemployment rates of the UI men in Farum and rest of Denmark resemble each other very closely and follow the business cycle. Hence, it is unlikely that Farum had a large labor market shock that affected its UI workers differently from those in the rest of Denmark.[12]

In Figure 5, we plot the arrest rates for no-UI and UI men. As we can see, the arrest rates for uninsured young men did not differ between Farum and the rest of Denmark until 1987. Thereafter, we see the arrest rate for the rest of Denmark starting to increase, whereas the rate for Farum remained constant. The gap between Farum and the rest of Denmark lasted until around 1998, when the arrest rate for the rest of Denmark started to drop to the level of Farum. We do not see any large discrepancy between the rates of UI men until 1998, and the subsequent increase in the arrest rate in Farum afterwards was

---

[12]Especially because the unemployment insurance policy at the national level is administered uniformly in all municipalities. The workfare requirement for the UI group was strengthened in late 1990s, but even then the passive period before activation lasted for one year.

due to an increase in violent crime. In contrast, the time-series pattern of the property crime arrest rate for Farum is close to that for the rest of Denmark.[13]

The divergence in the unemployment and arrest rates between Farum and the rest of Denmark is seen only for the uninsured. Farum only instituted the aggressive activation policy for the uninsured. The policies related to the insured were very similar to those for the rest of Denmark. Hence, we suspect that the relative decline in arrest rates among the uninsured men in Farum from around 1987 onward was primarily caused by the decline in unemployment rates induced by the aggressive activation policies.

However, there could be other explanations. One possibility is that during the policy period, the composition of the unemployment uninsured group in Farum diverged dramatically from that of the rest of Denmark, and thus their labor supply behavior diverged as well. To take such factors into account, we carefully control for observed characteristics, and also use fixed effects estimation when we econometrically evaluate the policy effect.

---

[13]The time-series figures for property crimes and violent crimes are available upon request.

4 Empirical Model

To evaluate the effects of policy reform in Farum, we use the following linear difference-in-differences model:

$$C_{it} = X_{it}\beta + \sum_{a=19}^{30} I_a(a_{it})\gamma_a + \sum_{y=1982}^{2005} I_y(t)\gamma_y + \sum_{m=2}^{12} I_m(t)\gamma_m \\ + \sum_{k=2}^{274} I_k(k_{it})\gamma_k + I_F(k_{it}) \times I_P(t)\delta + \epsilon_{it} \qquad (1)$$

where C_{it} is the number of arrests of individual i in period t, X_{it} is a number of different individual control variables, I_a is the age dummy for age a, I_y is the year dummy, I_m is the month dummy, and I_k is the municipality dummy, which equals 1 if individual i lives in municipality k in period t, i.e. if $k_{it} = k$, and 0 otherwise. I_F is the Farum dummy, which equals 1 if individual i lives in period t in Farum municipality, i.e. if $k_{it} = F$, and 0 otherwise. I_P is the policy dummy which equals 1 if the time period t belongs to the policy period in Farum, and 0 otherwise. The policy effect is identified by the parameter δ. We estimate equation 1 for the unemployment uninsured and insured separately. The OLS estimator of δ will then be unbiased if ϵ_{it} is orthogonal to $I_F \times I_P$.

Bertrand et al. (2004) argue that one tends to overreject the hypothesis of no policy effect in the difference-in-differences estimation if the serial correlation is not properly taken into account in deriving the standard errors of the parameter estimates. Furthermore, they show that in short panels, unless one has many local governments with differential timings of policy intervention, the problem persists even if the serial correlation is taken into account by using the robust procedures. Conley and Taber (2005) propose a method to conduct inference even in the above situation. In evaluating the Farum activation policy, we have only one single municipality that adopted an activation policy that was radically different from the policies of other municipalities. But we are still able to consistently estimate the standard errors using robust procedures due to the large time series sample size of $(2005 - 1981) \times 12 = 288$, which is divided between either 168 or 120 policy periods (1987-2001 or 1987-1997) and the remaining non-policy periods. In evaluating the national activation policy, we have both a large time series dimension and municipality-level variation in timing of policy adoption. We use robust procedures to derive the standard error.

The above OLS estimation is subject to two sources of bias. First, those who were uninsured could have changed their status from uninsured to insured during the policy period to avoid the possibility of activation. Indeed, later we present evidence that during the policy period, the level of UI membership in Farum relative to that of the rest of

Empirical model

Denmark was higher than in other periods. However, this endogeneity bias would reduce the estimated policy effect for the no-UI men in Farum, since the individuals who would switch from no-UI to UI status during the policy period would be those who were more likely to have better labor market prospects and be less criminally inclined than those who did not. Thus, the OLS policy effect would be a conservative estimate. On the other hand, the same switch in UI status would increase the arrest rate of the UI men during the policy period, which would bias their policy effect estimates upwards. This could partially explain the positive policy effect for the UI group that we will report later.

Second, individuals who were more criminally inclined could have left Farum during the policy period, which could have been the reason for the reduction in arrests in Farum during the policy period. This is a more serious issue, because *a priori* we cannot be sure of the direction of the bias. To deal with it, we first estimate the difference-in-differences model with fixed effects and then explicitly model the location decision. That is, we add fixed effects to the above equation as follows:

$$C_{it} = X_{it}\beta + \sum_{a=19}^{30} I_a(a_{it})\gamma_a + \sum_{y=1982}^{2005} I_y(t)\gamma_y + \sum_{m=2}^{12} I_m(t)\gamma_m \\ + \sum_{k=2}^{274} I_k(k_{it})\gamma_k + I_F(k_{it}) \times I_P(t)\delta + \alpha_i + \epsilon_{it} \quad (2)$$

The fixed effects estimator then will be unbiased if

$$E\left[\epsilon_{it}|I_P(t)=1, I_F(k_{it})=1, X\right] - E\left[\epsilon_{it}|I_P(t)=0, I_F(k_{it})=1, X\right] \\ - \{E\left[\epsilon_{kt}|I_P(t)=1, I_F(k_{it})=0, X\right] - E\left[\epsilon_{kt}|I_P(t)=0, I_F(k_{it})=0, X\right]\} = 0$$

and biased if LHS is non-zero, which could occur if people who left Farum during the policy period committed more crimes afterwards, and if people who came to Farum during the policy period committed more crimes before, even after controlling for Farum and time dummies - that is, if the time-varying component of the error term of the crime equation is correlated with Farum dummy.

We use the Heckman sample selection procedure to formally deal with the selection issue (Heckman, 1979). That is, we run the following first stage probit:

$$\Pr\left(I_F(k_{it})=1|Z_{it}\right) = \Phi\left(\theta Z_{it}\right) \quad (3)$$

where Z_{it} includes constant term, X_{it}, age and time dummies and a dummy indicating whether both parents live in Farum or not. Then, we estimate the following second stage regression model:

$$C_{it} = X_{it}\beta + \sum_{a=19}^{30} I_a(a_{it})\gamma_a + \sum_{y=1982}^{2005} I_y(t)\gamma_y + \sum_{m=2}^{12} I_m(t)\gamma_m + \sum_{k=2}^{274} I_k(k_{it})\gamma_k$$
$$+ \lambda_1(Z_{it}) I_F(k_{it})\gamma_{F1} + \lambda_2(Z_{it})(1 - I_F(k_{it}))\gamma_{F2}$$
$$+ I_F(k_{it}) \times I_P(t)\delta + \alpha_i + \varepsilon_{it} \qquad (4)$$

where

$$\lambda_1(Z_{it}) = \frac{\phi(\theta Z_{it})}{\Phi(\theta Z_{it})}, \quad \lambda_2(Z_{it}) = \frac{\phi(\theta Z_{it})}{1 - \Phi(\theta Z_{it})}$$

are the inverse Mill's ratios used to correct for the endogeneity bias due to selection.

The exclusion restriction is that whether both parents live in Farum or not affects the decision of individuals to live in Farum or elsewhere, but not their decision to commit crime. This could be violated when criminally inclined children leave Farum to avoid activation and parents follow, or when parents of criminally-active children are on welfare themselves and leave Farum to avoid activation. To minimize bias due to those possibilities, we only choose children who have at least one parent who is an UI member. We believe that these parents would have been working in a regular job most of the time, which makes it more likely that their location choices primarily depended on the job requirement and were not based on the location of their children, and also that they would have been less likely to be eligible for welfare payments. Another possible way in which parental location could affect criminal behavior of children is that children may reduce their criminal activity when they are living with parents. To control for this, we include in the RHS of the second stage regression equation dummies indicating whether children were living with their parents, and whether they were living in the same municipality as their parents, which should also partially control for the remaining endogeneity bias when children left Farum to avoid activation and parents followed to live together with them, even if the exclusion restriction for it does not hold perfectly.

Next, we discuss the empirical specification we use to estimate the policy effect at the national level. Strict activation policy was introduced gradually in Denmark during the 90s, starting with policies directed at younger age groups. In principle, this would enable us to estimate the policy effect separately from the time trend. We use the following linear difference-in-differences model:

Empirical model

$$C_{it} = X_{it}\beta + \sum_{a=19}^{35} I_a(a_{it})\gamma_a + \sum_{y=1982}^{2005} I_y(t)\gamma_y + \sum_{k=2}^{274} I_k(k_{it})\gamma_k$$
$$+ \left[I_{a\in\{18,19\}}(a_{it}) \times I_{t\geq 1990:7}(t)\right]\delta_1 + \left[I_{a\in\{20\}}(a_{it}) \times I_{t\geq 1991:10}(t)\right]\delta_2 \quad (5)$$
$$+ \left[I_{a\in\{21,24\}}(a_{it}) \times I_{t\geq 1994:7}(t)\right]\delta_3 + \left[I_{a\in\{25,29\}}(a_{it}) \times I_{t\geq 1998}(t)\right]\delta_4$$
$$+ \left[I_{a\in\{18,19\}}(a_{it}) \times I_{1990}(t)\right]\eta_1 + \left[I_{a\in\{20\}}(a_{it}) \times I_{1990}(t)\right]\eta_2 + \epsilon_{it}$$

$I_{a\in\{18,19\}}(a_{it})$ equals 1 if individual i in period t is either 18 or 19 years old, and 0 otherwise. $I_{t\geq 1990:7}(t)$ equals 1 if period t is later than or equal to July 1990, and 0 otherwise. The parameter δ_1 estimates the policy effect of the 1990 reform for the 18 to 19 age group. Similarly, δ_2 estimates the policy effect of 1991 reform for the 20 years age group, δ_3 the policy effect of the 1994 reform for the 21-24 years age group, and δ_4 the policy effect of the 1998 reform for the 25-29 years age group. We also estimate the above equation using fixed effects regression. We additionally include two interaction terms, namely the year 1990 dummy interacted with the age 18-19 dummy and with the age 20 dummy. These age groups had their policy reform around year 1990, when the monthly arrest data we used switched from those constructed using the predicted arrest date to the ones using the actual arrest date. The interaction terms are included to control for the irregularities in the arrest data in 1990 resulting from this switch.

There are several caveats to the estimation strategy. First, since the actual implementation of the activation policies for welfare participants was left to the municipalities, there were lags in the introduction of the reforms in many municipalities and also large differences in the level of strictness of the activation rules across municipalities. While many municipalities had rules that were less strict than the national ones, others, such as Farum had much tougher activation policies.

Second, since the reforms started with those for younger individuals, and the ones for older individuals followed later, most of the cohorts were either never subject to the tougher national rules or were subject to them at all ages up until the age of 29. Hence, for the cohorts that were subject to reforms, fixed effects would only capture the over-age differences in policy effect.

To address these issues, we also estimate the model by using the municipality-level differences in activation policy as the policy variation. For the period from 1994, the Danish Register includes detailed data on the starting and ending dates of each type of welfare spell, including whether it is a passive spell or an active spell involving a training program or a job placement program. From the data, we extract spells of welfare which ended up in activation and predict the length of spells until activation, and then use these spells as the municipality-level measure of the strictness of the activation policy. We do this separately for each year from 1994 - the start of the data - until 2002. To derive the spell, we look at the welfare data from year t until year $t+2$ and choose welfare spells that started in year t and were activated before the end of year $t+2$. The passive welfare spells that resulted in neither regular employment nor activation before $t+2$ represented in almost all municipalities less than 2% of all the passive spells that did not result in regular employment. Therefore, we conclude that bias due to right censoring can be ignored.

We then run the following regression:

$$S_{it} = \sum_{g=1}^{4} I_{A_g}(a_{it})\alpha_{gt} + \sum_{k=2}^{274} I_k(k_{it})\alpha_{kt} + \epsilon_{it} \quad (6)$$

S_{it} is months on welfare until the start of activation for spells beginning in year t for individual i. I_{A_g} is the dummy for the age group A_g. We have four age groups: below or equal to age 20 years group A_1, 21-24 years age group A_2, 25-29 years age group A_3, and 30-35 years age group A_4. The predicted municipality-level enforcement for an individual of age a, living in municipality k in year t is

$$\hat{S}(a,k,t) = \sum_{g=1}^{4} I_{A_g}(a)\hat{\alpha}_{gt} + \sum_{k=2}^{274} I_k(k)\hat{\alpha}_{kt}$$

Then, we use the predicted spell as the policy variable indicating municipality-level enforcement. That is, we estimate the following regression:

$$C_{it} = X_{it}\beta + \sum_{a=19}^{35} I_a(a_{it})\gamma_a + \sum_{y=1982}^{2005} I_y(t)\gamma_y \\ + \sum_{k=2}^{274} I_k(k_{it})\gamma_k + \hat{S}(a_{it},k_{it},t)\gamma_S + \epsilon_{it} \quad (7)$$

Notice that there are two sources of identification. The first source is the change over time in age coefficients of the predicted municipality-level enforcement, and the second is the change over time in the coefficients of the municipality dummies in the enforcement equation. The implicit assumption is similar to the difference-in-differences assumption that the effects of time series variation in age and the municipality specific effects come from the changes in enforcement.

5 Estimation Results

5.1 Results Based on the Reform in Farum

We present the estimation results in which we use the radical activation reform introduced in Farum in 1987 as the exogenous variation. We first divide the policy period into three. The first period is from 1987 to 1990, the second period from 1991 to 1997, and the third from 1998 to 2001. We consider the 1987 − 1990 period as being the introductory phase of the reform, and the 1991 − 1997 period as the fully implemented policy period. As we mentioned earlier, the requirement that all welfare recipients who did not get a job had to report to the Production House was only implemented from 1990. Finally, we consider the 1998 − 2001 period as being the ending period of the policy where the Farum activation policy and the national level policy started to converge.

In Table 2, we report the policy effects on arrest rate for the no-UI men between the ages of 18 and 30, estimated by OLS.[14] In the first result column (OLS1), we report the OLS results obtained when we separately estimate the policy effects of the three periods. We also consider two policy periods: one that starts in 1987 and ends in 2001, and the other that starts in 1987 and ends in 1997. We can see that men with more years of schooling, married men, and men with children were arrested less frequently. The higher education dummy, which equals one if the individual had qualification higher than high school and zero otherwise, has a positive coefficient estimate, but since the years of schooling effect dominates, the combined effect of additional years of schooling is negative. It is also interesting to see that the coefficient of the Danish/immigrants of Western origin dummy is insignificant. That is, when other characteristics are controlled for, non-Western immigrants did not get arrested significantly more often than the other men.[15]

The policy effect estimate is the coefficient for the interaction term of Farum and the policy period dummies. The policy is estimated to have a significant crime-reduction effect only for the full implementation period of 1991 − 97. Its policy effect is estimated to be quite large, i.e. it is estimated to reduce the arrest rate by 0.031 annually, which is a 33% reduction in the arrest rate relative to the mean arrest rate of no-UI men in Farum (see Table 1). In result columns 2 and 3 of Table 2, we present similar results where the policy period is set to be 1987 − 2001 and 1987 − 97 respectively. In both cases, policy effects are again estimated to be negative, statistically significant, and large, with an annual reduction by 0.017 arrests, i.e. a 17% reduction in annual arrest rate for the

---

[14]Significance levels for all tables are as follows: *,**,***; p <.05, .01, .001.

[15]The RHS variables include the age, year, month and municipality dummies, but we do not present the coefficient estimates for these due to space limitations.

Table 2: OLS and Fixed Effect for no-UI Men

Dependent Variable	OLS1 No. of Arrests	OLS2 No. of Arrests	OLS3 No. of Arrests	OLS4 No. of Arrests	FE1 No. of Arrests	FE2 No. of Arrests	FE3 No. of Arrests	FE4 No. of Arrests
Years of School	−0.00294 (0.00021**)	−0.00294 (0.00021**)	−0.00294 (0.00021**)	−0.00245 (0.00016**)	0.00048 (0.00018**)	0.00048 (0.00018**)	0.00047 (0.00018**)	0.00047 (0.00018**)
Higher Education	0.00294 (0.00057**)	0.00293 (0.00057**)	0.00293 (0.00057**)	0.00386 (0.00065**)	0.00179 (0.00073**)	0.00179 (0.00073**)	0.00180 (0.00073**)	0.00178 (0.00072**)
Married	−0.00168 (0.00091*)	−0.00167 (0.00090*)	−0.00167 (0.00091*)	−0.00100 (0.00088*)	0.00185 (0.00077**)	0.00187 (0.00077**)	0.00187 (0.00077**)	0.00185 (0.00077**)
Children	−0.00230 (0.00060**)	−0.00231 (0.00060**)	−0.00231 (0.00060**)	−0.00195 (0.00065**)	−0.00089 (0.00058)	−0.00090 (0.00058)	−0.00089 (0.00058)	−0.00092 (0.00058)
Danish or Western	0.00054 (0.00099)	0.00053 (0.00099)	0.00054 (0.00099)	0.00326 (0.00097**)				
Earnings				−0.00045 (0.00005**)				0.00001 (0.00002)
[87 − 90] × Far	−0.00116 (0.00091)			−0.00128 (0.00088)	−0.00156 (0.00126)			−0.00154 (0.00126)
Annual [91 − 97] × Far	−0.01392 (0.00262)			−0.01536 (0.00252)	−0.01969 (0.00376)			−0.01856 (0.00375)
Annual [98 − 01] × Far	−0.03149 (0.00044**)			−0.03028 (0.00042**)	−0.04512 (0.00142**)			−0.04496 (0.00142**)
Annual [87 − 01] × Far	0.00072 (0.00067)			0.00060 (0.00068)	−0.00102 (0.00104)			−0.00104 (0.00104)
Annual	0.00864			0.00715	−0.00147 (0.01220)			−0.00147 (0.01248)
[87 − 90] × Far Annual		−0.00140 (0.00039**)				−0.00220 (0.00106**)		
		−0.01678				−0.02636		
[87 − 97] × Far Annual			−0.00223 (0.00061**)				−0.00252 (0.00111**)	
			−0.02679				−0.03022	
R Squares	0.0054	0.0054	0.0054	0.0069				
ρ	0.0552	0.0548	0.0551	0.0543	−0.0073	−0.0074	−0.0073	−0.0073
Sample Size	799,401	799,401	799,401	798,972	799,401	799,401	799,401	798,972

Note: Standard errors are in parentheses.

1987 − 01 policy period and a 0.027 (28 %) annual reduction for the 1987 − 97 policy period. In all three specifications, the autocorrelation of the error term (ρ) is estimated to be small, around 0.055. Hence, the problem of autocorrelation in the error term raised by Bertrand et al. (2004) does not seem to arise in our results.

In Table 2, we also report the fixed effects results. Note that the coefficients for years of schooling and for the higher education and married dummies are positive and significant. Only the coefficient for the having children dummy is negative and insignificant. Imai and Krishna (2004) estimated the dynamic model of criminal decision on life cycle data of arrests. They concluded that it is highly criminal individuals who tend to reduce their criminal activities more after the age of 18. Since individual specific factors are averaged out and only the change in crime is left in the dependent variable, our results are consistent with those of Imai and Krishna (2004) when the criminals considered are those with low education and/or who are single. The estimated policy effects are similar to those of the OLS in the same table. That is, if we divide the policy periods into three sub-periods, the policy effects of the 1987 − 90 and 1998 − 2001 periods are estimated to be negative but insignificant, but that of the full implementation period, 1991 − 97, is estimated to be negative and significant, resulting in an annual reduction in arrests by 0.045, a 47% reduction. If we set the policy period to be 1987−2001, then the policy effect is significant and reduces the annual arrest rate by 0.0264 (27%), and for the 1987 − 97 policy period the effect is again significant and the annual reduction is estimated to be 0.030 (31%). Again, the autocorrelation of the error term is estimated to be small in all three specifications.

The estimated policy effect could be due to an increase in income because of transition into employment, or because individuals who work in workfare jobs may receive slightly higher earnings than the money they receive during passive welfare spells. In result column 4 and 8 of Table 2, we show the OLS and FE results obtained when we control for earnings.[16] In the OLS results, the coefficient for earnings is estimated to be negative and significant, while it is insignificant for the FE results. The policy effects are estimated to be very close to those obtained when earnings is not controlled for. Therefore, we conclude that the reduction in crime during the policy period is not likely to be due to an increase in earnings. Controlling for gross income instead of earnings yields similar results. Moreover, as we shall see below crime is reduced the most for men with onlye very little employment, and no-UI individuals enrolled in the Farum program did not earn

---

[16]The register data only show income at the annual level. Using annual earnings as a RHS variable for the regression for monthly criminal behavior is subject to measurement error bias. Still, income is likely to be correlated with employment status, and thus could be subject to the same endogeneity issue as the relationship between employment and crime. We take a closer look at this below where we show that the biggest crime reduction is found for men with practically no employment records.

more than unemployed elsewhere. Figure 8 in appendix shows annual level of earnings, gross income, and social benefits for individuals with at least 75% public dependency a given year. The figure gives no indication of an income rise due to the policy.[17]

The reduction in arrests for the young no-UI men during the policy period could be due to changes in Farum that is unrelated to the activation policy. These might be, for example, an increase in police spending in Farum, or an increase in municipal spending on youth activities. To take account of that possibility, we next run the same regressions for the young insured men. If, during the policy period, crime decreased for the uninsured but not for the insured, then we can rule out the effect of policies that affect both insured and uninsured.

In the first 4 results columns of Table 3, we report the results of the OLS estimation exercises for the UI men. The individual observables have coefficient estimates similar to those for the no-UI men. Apart from the higher education dummy, all the coefficients are negative, and significant at the 5% level except for the native Danish and Western immigrant dummy. Even though the coefficient for the higher education dummy is positive, it is insignificant, and its value is so small that the overall schooling effect is negative. On the other hand, the policy effects are very different from those of the no-UI men. In result column 1, we can see that the policy effect of all the sub-periods - the introductory period of 1987 − 90, the fully implemented period of 1991 − 97, and the ending period 1998 − 2001 are all positive, and significant for the 1991 − 97 and 1998 − 01 periods. The policy effect estimate for the 1987 − 01 period is also positive and significant, and even though that of the 1987 − 97 policy period is negative, its absolute value is small and insignificant. As we see from result column 4, the results are essentially the same when we control for income. In sum, we do not see any evidence of a negative policy effect for the insured men.

Similar results are confirmed for FE (also in Table 3), where we report the fixed effects estimates for the UI men, using the same model specification as that for the no-UI men. The autocorrelations of the error terms are also estimated to be small for both OLS and FEl, so that we can rule out the possibility of a serious downward bias in the standard errors of the coefficient estimates.[18]

---

[17]The erratic movement of the Farum graphs around 2001-2002 is caused by errors in registration of welfare; all payments are registered as zero in Statistics Denmarks register. The figures do not reflect the actual income for individuals in Farum for those two years. We used separate dummy-interaction between the two years and living in Farum to take this into account. The figure for the entire sample also yields no indication of any form of income shock in Farum, and is available from the authors upon request.

[18]As another robustness check, we estimated the regular and fixed effects logit models. The policy effects have the same sign and significance as those of the OLS for regular logit models, but the logit models with fixed effect failed to converge. Those results be obtained from the authors on request.

Table 3: OLS and Fixed Effect for the UI Men

	OLS1	OLS2	OLS3	OLS4	FE1	FE2	FE3	FE4
Dependent Variable	No. of Arrests	No. of Arrests	No. of Arrests	No. of Arrests	No. of Arrests	No. of Arrests	No. of Arrests	No. of Arrests
Years of School	−0.00092	−0.00092	−0.00092	−0.000831	0.00004	0.00004	0.00004	0.00005
	(0.00009**)	(0.00009**)	(0.00009**)	(0.00010**)	(0.00016)	(0.00016)	(0.00016)	(0.00016)
Higher Education	0.00009	0.00009	0.00009	0.00039	0.00088	0.00088	0.00088	0.00093
	(0.00024)	(0.00024)	(0.00024)	(0.00027)	(0.00064)	(0.00064)	(0.00064)	(0.00064)
Married	−0.00062	−0.00061	−0.00061	−0.00037	0.00074	0.00074	0.00074	0.00076
	(0.00017**)	(0.00017**)	(0.00017**)	(0.00016**)	(0.00022**)	(0.00022**)	(0.00022**)	(0.00022**)
Children	−0.00105	−0.00105	−0.00105	−0.00095	−0.00070	−0.00070	−0.00070	−0.00070
	(0.00017**)	(0.00017**)	(0.00017**)	(0.00017**)	(0.00021**)	(0.00021**)	(0.00021**)	(0.00021**)
Western	−0.00058	−0.00060	−0.00060	−0.00085				
	(0.00056)	(0.00056)	(0.00056)	(0.00051*)				
Earnings				−0.00023				−0.00003
				(0.00002**)				(0.00001**)
$[87-90] \times Far$	0.00017			0.00028	0.00065			0.00067
	(0.00024)			(0.00024)	(0.00078)			(0.00079)
Annual	0.00208			0.00333	0.00779			0.00807
$[91-97] \times Far$	0.00043			0.0004	0.00042			0.00045
	(0.00018**)			(0.00018**)	(0.00064)			(0.00064)
Annual	0.00516			0.00532	0.00502			0.00540
$[98-01] \times Far$	0.00140			0.00124	0.00050			0.00050
	(0.00027**)			(0.00027**)	(0.00082)			(0.00082)
Annual	0.01675			0.01488	0.00595			0.00600
$[87-01] \times Far$		0.00055				0.00053		
		(0.00015**)				(0.00058)		
Annual		0.00659				0.00421		
$[87-97] \times Far$			−0.00003				0.00035	
			(0.00017)				(0.00054)	
Annual			−0.00035				0.00421	
R Squares	0.0030	0.0030	0.0030	0.0039				
ρ	0.0190	0.0190	0.0190	0.0181	−0.0192	−0.0192	−0.0192	−0.0191
Sample Size	1,358,309	1,358,309	1,358,309	1,358,287	1,358,309	1,358,309	1,358,309	1,358,287

Note: Standard errors are in parentheses

Two types of endogeneity could bias the fixed effects estimation of the policy effect. First, in order to avoid activation when unemployed, individuals might seek jobs and join an UI fund. In Figure 6 we plot the proportions of men aged 18-30 who were insured in Farum and in the rest of Denmark. We can see that a smaller fraction of young men were insured in Farum than in the rest of Denmark, and that the difference slowly increased over time until 1990, from 0.130 in 1986 to 0.172 in 1990. After that, it decreased until 1995 when it reached a level of 0.075, where after it began to increase again.

Figure 6: Share with UI membership, 18- to 30-year old men, 1981-2005

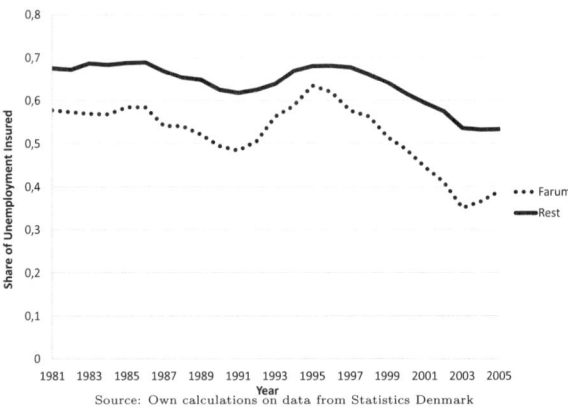

Source: Own calculations on data from Statistics Denmark

In Table 4, we report the results of the probit analysis, which estimates the insurance choice probability. There, after controlling for the observables such as age, education, marital status, children, year and Farum residence, it is estimated that during the policy period, the interaction term of Farum and policy period dummies was positive and significant at the 5% level for the 1990-97 and 1987-2001 policy periods and significant at the 10% level for the 1987-97 policy period. Because the individuals who can find jobs and join an UI fund are the stronger workers and therefore less criminally active, the decrease in the proportion of uninsured individuals in Farum during the policy period should have increased the crime rate among its uninsured individuals. Thus, the insurance choice would bias the policy parameter estimates towards zero. Hence, the negative policy effect we obtain is likely to be a conservative estimate. On the other hand, individuals who switched their status from no-UI to UI during the policy period may have been the more criminally active among the insured, and thus may have increased the arrest rate for the UI-men during the policy period. This could be the reason for the slightly positive and sometimes significant policy effects estimated by OLS and the Fixed Effects for the UI men.

Estimation results

Table 4: Probit Estimation for Insurance Choice

	Probit1		Probit2		Probit3	
Dependent Variable	UI		UI		UI	
Years of Schooling	−0.0526	(0.0041**)	−0.0526	(0.0041**)	−0.0526	(0.0041**)
Higher Education	0.8365	(0.0202**)	0.8365	(0.0202**)	0.8366	(0.0202**)
Married	0.0237	(0.0182)	0.0236	(0.0182)	0.0239	(0.0182)
Children	0.2549	(0.0158**)	0.2554	(0.0158**)	0.2556	(0.0158**)
Western or Danish	0.0838	(0.0296**)	0.0834	(0.0296**)	0.0829	(0.0296**)
Farum	−0.2985	(0.0243**)	−0.2986	(0.0243**)	−0.2818	(0.0218**)
$[87-90] \times Farum$	−0.0018	(0.0332)				
$[91-97] \times Farum$	0.1296	(0.0373**)				
$[98-01] \times Farum$	0.0639	(0.0403)				
$[87-01] \times Farum$			0.0657	(0.0285**)		
$[87-97] \times Farum$					0.0493	(0.0276*)
Sample Size	2,157,710		2,157,710		2,157,710	

Note: Standard errors are in parentheses.

Another potential source of bias would arise when, during the policy period, young uninsured men left or stayed out of Farum for fear of activation. Here, we cannot *a priori* assess whether individuals who left or stayed out of Farum would be more criminally active or not. Hence, we use the Heckman two-step approach to estimate jointly the location and the criminal choice.

In Tables 5, 6 and 13, we report the results of the Heckman two-step estimation. In the second column of Table 5, we present the parameter estimates of the first stage probit model of whether or not to live in Farum for the no-UI men.[19] Parents living outside Farum has a negative effect significant at the 5% level. Parents living in Farum has a positive significant effect at the 10% level. That is, instruments are significant in explaining Farum residence. In Table 6, we report the second step fixed effects results for the uninsured. The coefficient for the inverse Mill's ratio term, representing the selection bias for the arrest rate in Farum, is estimated to be negative, and that for the arrest rate in the rest of Denmark is estimated to be positive, which implies downward bias of the fixed effects estimation without selection bias correction. If we compare the estimated policy effects of Table 6 with those of Table 2, we can see that all the coefficients are similar in magnitude except for those of the policy periods 1987 − 90, 1998 − 2001, and 1987 − 1997, where the sample-selection-corrected policy-effect estimates are smaller in magnitude than those of the uncorrected fixed effects for the first two policy periods, and the corrected estimates larger than the uncorrected ones for the third policy period. Notice that the sample-selection correction did not always result in a decrease in the estimated

---

[19]We included year and age dummies in the RHS, but we do not report their coefficient estimates to save space. Since residence information is only reported annually, we did not include month dummies.

Table 5: Heckman Two-step Estimation, 1st Step, no-UI

Dependent Variable	Farum	
Years of Schooling	−0.03427	(0.00980**)
Higher Education	0.11014	(0.04904**)
Married	0.16269	(0.06083**)
Children	0.29229	(0.04724**)
Parents outside Farum	−1.93635	(0.04305**)
Parents in Farum	0.09409	(0.04851*)
Sample Size	499, 410	

Note: Standard errors are in parentheses.

policy effect. This is because of the difference in the sample used in the estimation. For the two-step estimation, we only use individuals who had at least one parent who was unemployment insured.

Note that the effect of living together with parents is negative and significant at the 10% level for all specifications, whereas the effect of living in the same municipality with parents is positive but insignificant.

In the Heckman two-step procedure for the UI men we do not see any negative policy effect, which again excludes any possibility of exogenous changes in Farum having a noticeable impact in reducing crime for both the insured and uninsured during the policy period (see Table 13 in the Appendix).[20]

5.2 Direct and Indirect Effects of Activation

So far, we have reported results that indicate that ALMPs for no-UI young men in Farum were effective in reducing their crime rate. The next issue we address is why that was. We consider two reasons for it; an indirect and a direct. Activation could have induced welfare recipients to take up regular employment, which might have reduced crime. We have already seen that an increase in average income from activation is not likely to have been a contributing factor behind the policy effect. Still, the policy could have induced certain types of men to take up employment, reducing their crime as a consequence. There is a large literature documenting that employment decreases crime. This would be an indirect effect of activation. A direct effect would be when activation reduces the number of crimes committed by individuals who remain on welfare and hence in the activation program, and such effects have not been investigated much in the literature.

[20]If we include annual income in the RHS of both the two steps, the estimated policy effects have the right sign but are insignificant for the unemployment uninsured (due to smaller sample size as discussed above). The policy effects are insignificant for the unemployment insured. These results are available from the authors on request. The sample selection correction terms are insignificant as well, implying insignificant sample-selection-bias.

Table 6: Heckman Two-Step Estimation, 2nd Step, no-UI

	FE1	FE2	FE3
Dependent Variable	No. of Arrests	No. of Arrests	No. of Arrests
Years of Schooling	0.00074	0.00075	0.00075
	(0.00027**)	(0.00027**)	(0.00027**)
Higher Education	0.00189	0.00188	0.00191
	(0.00092**)	(0.00092**)	(0.00092**)
Married	−0.00023	−0.00021	−0.00022
	(0.00095)	(0.00096)	(0.00096)
Children	−0.00166	−0.00168	−0.00168
	(0.00085**)	(0.00085**)	(0.00085**)
Parents same Home	−0.00139	−0.00138	−0.00138
	(0.00081*)	(0.00081*)	(0.00081*)
Parents same Muni.	0.00149	0.00148	0.00147
	(0.00092)	(0.00092)	(0.00092)
Inverse Mill's Ratio λ_1	−0.00861	−0.00871	−0.00881
	(0.00642)	(0.00642)	(0.00642)
Inverse Mill's Ratio λ_2	0.00930	0.00954	0.00948
	(0.00489*)	(0.00485**)	(0.00490*)
$[87-90] \times$ Farum	−0.00125		
	(0.00168)		
annual	−0.01499		
$[91-97] \times$ Farum	−0.00427		
	(0.00166**)		
annual	−0.05124		
$[98-01] \times$ Farum	−0.00037		
	(0.00152)		
annual	−0.00445		
$[87-01] \times$ Farum		−0.00206	
		(0.00128)	
annual		−0.02477	
$[87-97] \times$ Farum			−0.00297
			(0.00134**)
annual			−0.03568

Note: Standard errors are in parentheses. Sample size is 499,410.

In Table 7, we present OLS results of the effects of activation policy reform in Farum where we control for the fraction of days in a month on welfare. We derive this information from the data on monthly welfare benefit payments, which are available for the period 1984 - 2005. Due to space limitations, we only report the coefficient estimates of the policy effects.

We can see that the receipt of welfare benefits increased crime significantly, both for the uninsured and the insured, and that the direct policy effect was negative and significant for the full implementation policy period of 1991 − 97 and for the 1987 − 97 period for the uninsured, but positive for the insured. Note that there are individuals who are registered as being unemployment insured in the data, and still received welfare

Table 7: Controlling for Welfare

Dependent Variable: No. of Arrests				
	Non-UI, OLS	UI, OLS	Non-UI, FE	UI, FE
Welfare	0.02481	0.01474	0.00782	0.00339
	(0.00206**)	(0.00087**)	(0.00080**)	(0.00086**)
[87 − 90]×Farum	−0.00180	0.00054	−0.00107	0.00102
	(0.00117)	(0.00026**)	(0.00139)	(0.00074)
[91 − 97]×Farum	−0.00176	0.00082	−0.00261	0.00097
	(0.00076**)	(0.00018**)	(0.00155*)	(0.00069)
[98 − 01]×Farum	0.00204	0.00152	0.00019	0.00095
	(0.00060**)	(0.00025**)	(0.00152)	(0.00086)
R Squares	0.0132	0.0048		
ρ	0.0443	0.0258	-0.0062	-0.0138
Welfare	0.02480	0.01474	0.00782	0.00339
	(0.00206**)	(0.00087**)	(0.00080**)	(0.00086**)
[87 − 01]×Farum	−0.00089	0.00088	−0.0012	0.00099
	(0.00067)	(0.00016**)	(0.0012)	(0.00060*)
R Squares	0.0132	0.0048		
ρ	0.0439	0.0258	-0.0064	-0.0138
Welfare	0.02480	0.01474	0.00782	0.00339
	(0.00206**)	(0.00087**)	(0.00080**)	(0.00086**)
[87 − 97]×Farum	−0.00248	0.00017	−0.00205	0.00061
	(0.00096**)	(0.00016)	(0.00120*)	(0.00054)
R Squares	0.0132	0.0048		
ρ	0.0442	0.0258	-0.0062	-0.0138
Sample Size	693,403	1,151,852	693,403	1,151,852

Note: Standard errors are in parentheses.

payments. Since the register data only contain information on unemployment insurance status at the end of the year, this could reflect a transition from no-UI to UI status during a year. But what is more important is that individuals need to be a UI member for at least one year before being eligible for UI payments. Those who are members of the UI Fund but are not yet eligible for the UI benefit and lost their job receive welfare benefits, but they were not subject to the tough activation policies implemented in Farum. That is to say, we compare the arrest rates of no-UI and UI recipients, where in both cases the welfare payments are controlled for, but the tough activation rule only applied for the no-UI group. The fact that the interaction term of the policy period and Farum dummy is negative and statistically significant only for the non-UI recipients supports our claim that the tough activation policy was effective in reducing crime.

In Table 7, we also show the results for the fixed effects. The estimated policy effects have the same signs as the OLS estimates. However, the policy effects for no-UI for the 1991 − 97 and 1987 − 97 policy periods are only significant at the 10% level, and that for 1987 − 2001 policy period is insignificant. In Table 8, we present the OLS and fixed effects difference-in-difference-in-differences estimation for the policy effect, i.e., we identify the

Estimation results

Table 8: Controlling for Welfare, DDD

	OLS		FE	
Welfare	0.02257	(0.00168**)	0.00645	(0.00058**)
no-UI	0.00104	(0.00026**)	−0.00080	(0.00029**)
Farum × Non-UI	0.00158	(0.00040**)	0.00253	(0.00106**)
[87 − 90]×Farum	0.00043	(0.00051)	0.00032	(0.00082)
[87 − 90]×Farum × no-UI	−0.00176	(0.00009**)	−0.00068	(0.00140)
[91 − 97]×Farum	0.00092	(0.00027**)	0.00098	(0.00069)
[91 − 97]×Farum × no-UI	−0.00262	(0.00013**)	−0.00349	(0.00137**)
[98 − 01]×Farum	0.00220	(0.00033**)	0.00150	(0.00083*)
[98 − 01]×Farum × no-UI	−0.00115	(0.00008**)	−0.00241	(0.00149)
R-Squares	0.0107			
ρ	0.0204		−0.0164	
Welfare	0.02256	(0.00168**)	0.00645	(0.00058**)
no-UI	0.00104	(0.00025**)	−0.00081	(0.00029**)
no-UI × Farum	0.00158	(0.00040**)	0.00236	(0.00105**)
[87 − 01]×Farum	0.00104	(0.00026**)	0.00086	(0.00060*)
[87 − 01]×Farum × no-UI	−0.00199	(0.00008**)	−0.00218	(0.00114*)
R-Squares	0.0107		−0.0138	
ρ	0.0203		−0.0138	
Welfare	0.02256	(0.00168**)	0.00339	(0.00086**)
no-UI	0.00104	(0.00025**)	−0.00081	(0.00029**)
no-UI × Farum	0.00115	(0.00039**)	0.0058	(0.00089*)
[87 − 97]×Farum	−0.00005	(0.00038)	0.00011	(0.00055)
[87 − 97]×Farum × no-UI	−0.00186	(0.00012**)	−0.00141	(0.00110)
R-Squares	0.0107			
ρ	0.0204		−0.0164	
Sample Size	1,845,255		1,845,255	

Note: Standard errors are in parentheses.

policy effect for no-UI men relative to UI men. Thus, the policy effect is estimated by the coefficient of the interaction term of policy period dummy, the Farum dummy and the no-UI dummy. All the OLS policy effect estimates are negative and significant, and the FE estimated policy effect for the 1991 − 97 policy period is now negative and significant at the 5% level.

In Table 9, result column 1 (FE1) we report fixed effects results separately for uninsured young men who were on welfare more than 25% of the days in a month, and for less than or equal to 25% of the days in a month. Similarly, result column 2 (FE2) shows the results for 50% and result column 3 (FE3) for 75%. As we can see, the 1991 − 97 policy effect is estimated to be significant at the 5% level for a proportion of welfare days greater than 25%, 50% and 75%, and that of the 1987 − 2001 policy period is significant at the 10% level for all those cases. The estimated policy effects are very similar for all cases. We can see that the sample sizes of people who are on welfare for more than 25%, 50% and 75% of the time are very similar, which implies that people are either on welfare

Table 9: Fixed Effects for Unemployment Uninsured Individuals

		25 %	50 %	75 %
		FE1	FE2	FE3
	Dependent Variable	No. of Arrests	No. of Arrests	No. of Arrests
$> x\%$	$[87-90] \times Farum$	−0.0102 (0.0085)	−0.0102 (0.0085)	−0.0102 (0.0085)
	$[91-97] \times Farum$	−0.0204 (0.0097**)	−0.0204 (0.0097**)	−0.0204 (0.0097**)
	$[98-01] \times Farum$	−0.0125 (0.0101)	−0.0125 (0.0101)	−0.0125 (0.0101)
	ρ	0.2479	0.2479	0.2479
	$[87-01] \times Farum$	−0.0145 (0.0078*)	−0.0145 (0.0078*)	−0.0145 (0.0078*)
	ρ	0.2483	0.2483	0.2484
	$[87-97] \times Farum$	−0.0119 (0.0075)	−0.0119 (0.0075)	−0.0119 (0.0075)
	ρ	0.2496	0.2496	0.2496
	Sample Size	115,129	115,123	115,116
$\leq x\%$	$[87-90] \times Farum$	0.0004 (0.0010)	0.0004 (0.0010)	0.0004 (0.0010)
	$[91-97] \times Farum$	−0.0033 (0.0105)	−0.0033 (0.0105)	−0.0033 (0.0105)
	$[98-01] \times Farum$	0.0008 (0.0011)	0.0008 (0.0011)	0.0008 (0.0011)
	ρ	−0.0088	−0.0088	−0.0088
	$[87-01] \times Farum$	0.0003 (0.0008)	0.0003 (0.0005)	0.0003 (0.0008)
	ρ	−0.0089	−0.0089	−0.0089
	$[87-97] \times Farum$	−0.0003 (0.0008)	−0.0003 (0.0008)	−0.0003 (0.0008)
	ρ	−0.0089	−0.0089	−0.0089
	Sample Size	578,274	578,280	578,287

Note: Standard errors are in parentheses.

for less than one week in a month or almost on welfare the entire month. On the other hand, if we look at the policy effect for the no-UI men who are on welfare *less* than or equal to 25%, 50% and 75% of the time, then we can that none of the policy effects are significant.

If we multiply the policy coefficients by 12 to derive the annualized policy effect, for the $1991-97$ and $1987-2001$ policy periods we find that the decrease in the arrest rate is higher than the overall annual arrest rate of the no-UI, which is around 0.10 for Farum and 0.11 for the rest of Denmark. This results from the fact that people who are dependent on welfare had average annual arrest rates that were much higher than those for the rest of the unemployment uninsured men to begin with.

From these results we see that workfare policy is most effective in reducing crime for those individuals in Farum who are most frequently on welfare, and this is not due to higher payments to program participants. Recall from the previous section that welfare recipients in Farum did not experience an increase in income along with the introduction of the welfare regime; the contrary is actually the case (see Figure 8 in Appendix). The literature on program evaluation concludes that the individuals with the highest welfare dependency are the ones for whom ALMPs have the least employment effect. It also seems that these are the individuals who are most criminally active.

Table 10: Regression with National Data

	Unemployment Uninsured		Unemployment Insured	
	OLS	FE	OLS	FE
Policy$_{18,19}$	−0.00263	−0.00051	−0.00087	0.00029
	(0.00118**)	(0.00165)	(0.00187)	(0.00179)
Policy$_{20}$	−0.00472	−0.00146	−0.00145	−0.00027
	(0.00109**)	(0.00148)	(0.00144)	(0.00116)
Policy$_{21\sim24}$	−0.00313	0.00037	−0.00087	−0.00041
	(0.00070**)	(0.00107)	(0.00034**)	(0.00039)
Policy$_{25\sim29}$	−0.00390	0.00037	−0.00036	0.00018
	(0.00115**)	(0.00098)	(0.00018*)	(0.00025)
R squares	0.0058		0.0028	
ρ	0.0559	-0.0024	0.0197	-0.0143
Sample Size	719,202	719,202	1,663,254	1,663,254

Note: Standard errors are in parentheses
Policy$_{20\sim24} \equiv I\{age \in \{21,...,24\}\} \times \{t \geq 1994\}$,
Policy$_{25\sim29} \equiv I\{age \in \{25,...,29\}\} \times \{t \geq 1998\}$

By reaching out to individuals with very low chances of regular employment, ALMP improves life for the local community by reducing criminal activity among those who are the most likely to commit crimes.

5.3 Results Based on National Reforms

Next, we estimate the policy effect of the national reforms mandating a tougher activation requirement. In Table 10, we present the estimation results of equation 5. That is, we estimate the policy effect of the national reforms targeting 18- to 19-year-olds, 20-year-olds, 21- to 24-year-olds and the 25- to 29-year-olds. In result columns 1 and 2, we report the OLS and fixed effects estimates of the policy effect for the no-UI men, and in result columns 3 and 4, we show those for the insured men. As we can see, OLS estimated policy effects are negative and significant for the uninsured. They are negative for the insured but only significant for the 21- to 24-year-olds, and their magnitude is much smaller than that of the uninsured. On the other hand, none of the fixed effects policy effects are significant, and the ones for the older uninsured have the wrong sign. As we discussed earlier, the reason for the discrepancy between the OLS and FE results could be due to the fact that there were lags in enforcement of the policy reform, and given the timing of the reforms, some cohorts were subject to a tough activation policy at all ages, and other cohorts did not experience any changes in the activation policy at any age. Thus, the FE-estimated policy effect for the older uninsured individuals is nonnegative because it might only be measuring the marginal policy effect of additional activation at that age.

Table 11: Regression with National Data, Local Level Variation in Enforcement.

	Total		Weekend	
Non-UI	OLS	FE	OLS	FE
Policy	0.00376	0.00431	0.00064	0.00075
	(0.00220*)	(0.00122**)	(0.00043)	(0.00056)
R-Squares	0.0303		0.0135	
Sample Size	350,515	350,515	350,515	350,515
UI	OLS	FE	OLS	FE
Policy	0.00080	0.00031	0.00027	0.00008
	(0.00044*)	(0.00025)	(0.00014*)	(0.00013)
R-Squares	0.0174		0.0080	
Sample Size	849,024	849024	849,024	849,024
DDD	OLS	FE	OLS	FE
Policy	0.00592	0.00314	0.00120	0.00080
	(0.00086**)	(0.00067**)	(0.00026**)	(0.00031**)
R-Squares	0.0350		0.140	
Sample Size	1,199,539	1,199,539	1,199,539	1,199,539

Note: Standard errors are in parentheses.

In Table 11, we present the estimation results of equation 7, where we use the predicted length of welfare spell until activation at the municipality level as policy variation. The OLS estimates for the no-UI men are positive and significant at a the 10% level for the uninsured. The positive coefficient estimate is expected because shorter spells means stronger enforcement. For the insured, the coefficient is positive and significant at the 10% level but much smaller than that of the uninsured. The fixed effects estimate is positive and significant at the 5% level for the uninsured and insignificant for the insured.[21] It is important to note that the local variation in enforcement of the activation rule may not be exogenous. It may very well be correlated with the local level unemployment rate or the budget at the local level. Therefore, the important finding here is that there is a significant difference of the policy effect between the no-UI and UI workers. The DDD estimates of the policy effect are positive and significant both for OLS and FE.[22]

---

[21] Here we have used the annual data constructed from the monthly data. We did this because in this case the policy variable is annual, and since we have the municipality level policy variation for each year for 274 municipalities, we are not subject to the potential problems in obtaining the standard errors in difference-in-differences estimation discussed in Bertrand et al. (2004) and Conley and Taber (2005) even when the time series sample size is small. The aggregation over 12 month seems to improve the accuracy of the parameter estimates by removing the large monthly variations in crime. When we carried out the same exercise using the monthly data, the coefficient estimates were similar, but the standard errors were much larger, resulting in the FE estimates being insignificant. Those results are available from the authors on request.

[22] We also conducted the same estimation exercises with earnings as an additional RHS variable. The policy effects were estimated as being very similar to those reported. The results are available on request.

Estimation results

Finally, in result columns 3 and 4, we present the OLS, FE and DDD estimates where the dependent variable is weekend crime. For the uninsured individuals, both the OLS and the FE coefficients have the expected positive sign but are insignificant. The coefficients for the insured individuals are also positive but their magnitudes are much smaller than those of the uninsured. The DDD estimates of the policy effect, on the other hand, are positive and significant at the 5% level, both for the OLS and FE. Since we cannot argue convincingly any more that the policy variation for the no-UI is exogenous, the most credible evidence is that of the DDD which identifies the policy effect from the difference in the change in crime between the uninsured and insured. Therefore, we conclude that the activation policy not only reduces crime through the reduction in hours available for crime during weekdays, but also reduces the number of crimes committed during the weekends, which suggests that there are positive changes in attitudes or lifestyles of individuals, which influence weekend activities.

6 Concluding Remarks

We have estimated the effect of ALMPs on the criminal behavior of young men who are not insured against unemployment. We exploited two policy changes. First, we used a unique policy experiment that began in 1987 in Farum, where a 100% work or training requirement was imposed on all welfare recipients immediately from the date of enrollment. By comparing the changes in crime rates among the welfare recipients in Farum before and after 1987 with those of the rest of Denmark, we identified the effects of workfare on the crime rate. Second, we examined the effects of a series of national welfare reforms introduced during the 1990s. These reforms strengthened the work requirement for young welfare recipients and were introduced gradually, being applied first to the youngest welfare participants. The differential introduction of the workfare reform across different age groups worked as the exogenous policy variation. We estimated the policy effect by including the municipality-level variation in enforcement of the national policy.

We find that a tough work requirement reduces crime, and that the policy effect is both statistically and economically significant. We also find that the effect comes not only indirectly from the reduction in welfare participation but also from the reduced criminal activities of the individuals who are on welfare and are activated, and thus a direct effect of "being active" in itself for these young men. Furthermore, the significant policy effect on weekend crime indicates that the crime reduction is also a result of positive changes in attitude or even lifestyle, not just a reduction in the hours allocated to criminal activities. This suggests that the effect could be long lasting.

In Denmark and many other countries in Europe, ALMPs now cover most workers in the labor force when they are unemployed. Hence, it is fair to say that they affect a large fraction of the population. However, research on these policies has been almost exclusively focused on their effects on employment and wages. We believe that it is important that we also take a careful look at other aspects of activation policies that could be of importance for the general public, such as their effect on criminal behavior. An important issue that is left for future research is to investigate which programs work best in reducing the crime rate among young men. Our results suggest that activation programs that induce fewer threat effects (see Black et al., 2003) - and are less targeted towards immediate employment - could be more effective in reducing crimes among recipients, since the people affected most frequently by these programs are also the more criminally active welfare dependents. Given sufficiently strong crime reduction effects, such programs could be a better choice for the general public.

References

Bayer, P., R. Hjalmarsson, and D. Pozen (2009). Building criminal capital behind bars: Peer effects in juvenile corrections. *The Quarterly Journal of Economics 124*(1), 105–147.

Bertrand, M., E. Duflo, and S. Mullainathan (2004). How much should we trust Differences-in-Differences estimates? *The Quarterly Journal of Economics 119*(1), 249–275.

Besley, T. and S. Coate (1992). Workfare versus welfare: Incentive arguments for work requirements in Poverty-Alleviation programs. *The American Economic Review 82*(1), 249–261.

Besley, T. and S. Coate (1995). The design of income maintenance programmes. *The Review of Economic Studies 62*(2), 187–221.

Birkbak, B. (1997). *På med vanten! Moderne beskæftigelsespolitik i Farum. [Gloves on! Modern employment policies in Farum]*. Farum: Farums Arkiver og Museer.

Black, D. A., J. A. Smith, M. C. Berger, and B. J. Noel (2003). Is the threat of reemployment services more effective than the services themselves? evidence from random assignment in the UI system. *The American Economic Review 93*(4), 1313–1327.

Bolvig, I., P. Jensen, and M. Rosholm (2003). The employment effects of active social policy. IZA Discussion Papers 736, Institute for the Study of Labor (IZA),, Bonn.

Brogaard, S. and H. Weisse (1997). *Evaluering af Lov om kommunal aktivering: Kommuneundersøgelse [Evaluation of Law concerning municipal activation: Municipal inquiry]*. Copenhagen: The Danish National Institute for Social Research.

Cantor, D. and K. C. Land (1985). Unemployment and crime rates in the Post-World war II united states: A theoretical and empirical analysis. *American Sociological Review 50*(3), 317–332.

Chiricos, T. G. (1987). Rates of crime and unemployment: An analysis of aggregate research evidence. *Social Problems 34*(2), 187–212.

Conley, T. and C. Taber (2005). Inference with "Difference in differences" with a small number of policy changes. Technical Working Paper Series 312, National Bureau of Economic Research.

Donohue III, J. J. and P. Siegelman (1998). Allocating resources among prisons and social programs in the battle against crime. *The Journal of Legal Studies 27*(1), 1–43.

Foucault, M. (1975). *Surveiller et punir: Naissance de la Prison [Discipline and Punishment: The Birth of the Prison]*. Paris: Gallimard.

Fougére, D., F. Kramarz, and J. Pouget (2009). Youth unemployment and crime in france. *Journal of the European Economic Association 7*(5), 909–938.

Gould, E. D., B. A. Weinberg, and D. B. Mustard (2002). Crime rates and local labor market opportunities in the united states: 1979-1997. *Review of Economics and Statistics 84*(1), 45–61.

Graversen, B. (2004). *Employment effects of active labor market programs: Do the programs help welfare benefit recipients to find jobs?* Ph.D. thesis, Department of Economics, University of Aarhus, Denmark.

Heckman, J. J. (1979). Sample selection bias as a specification error. *Econometrica 47*(1), 153–161.

Heckman, J. J., R. J. Lalonde, and J. A. Smith (1999). The economics and econometrics of active labor market programs. In O. C. Ashenfelter and D. Card (Eds.), *Handbook of Labor Economics*, Volume 3, pp. 1865–2097. San Diego, CA: Elsevier.

Imai, S. and K. Krishna (2004). Employment, deterrence, and crime in a dynamic model. *International Economic Review 45*(3), 845–872.

Jacob, B. A. and L. Lefgren (2003). Are idle hands the devil's workshop? incapacitation, concentration, and juvenile crime. *The American Economic Review 93*(5), 1560–1577.

Kreiner, C. T. and T. Tranæs (2005). Optimal workfare with voluntary and involuntary unemployment. *The Scandinavian Journal of Economics 107*(3), 459–474.

Levitt, S. D. (2001). Alternative strategies for identifying the link between unemployment and crime. *Journal of Quantitative Criminology 17*(4), 377–390.

Lochner, L. (2011). Education policy and crime. In P. J. Cook, J. Ludwig, and J. McCrary (Eds.), *Controlling Crime: Strategies and Tradeoffs*. Chicago: University of Chicago Press.

Long, S. K. and A. D. Witte (1981). Current economic trends: implications for crime and criminal justice. In K. N. Wright (Ed.), *Crime and criminal justice in a declining economy*, pp. 69–143. Cambridge, MA: Oelschlager, Gunn and Hain.

References

Machin, S. and O. Marie (2006). Crime and benefit sanctions. *Portuguese Economic Journal 5*(2), 149–165.

Oster, A. and J. Agell (2007). Crime and unemployment in turbulent times. *Journal of the European Economic Association 5*(4), 752–775.

Parsons, D. O., T. Tranæs, and H. B. Lilleør (2003). Voluntary public unemployment insurance. CESifo Working Paper Series 1010, CESifo Group Munich.

Raphael, S. and R. Winter-Ebmer (2001). Identifying the effect of unemployment on crime. *Journal of Law & Economics 44*, 259–283.

Torfing, J. (1999). Workfare with welfare: Recent reforms of the danish welfare state. *Journal of European Social Policy 9*(1), 5–28.

Tranæs, T. and L. P. Geerdsen (2008). *Forbryderen og samfundet. Livsvilkår og uformel straf [The Criminal and Society: Living Conditions and Informal Punishment]*. København: Gyldendal.

Wilson, J. Q. (1983). *Thinking about crime*. New York: Basic Books.

A Appendix

Appendix

Table 12: Sample Statistics, National Data

	Total		no-UI		UI	
Variable	mean	sd	mean	sd	mean	sd
Unemployment Insured	0.708	0.455				
Annual Arrest Rate	0.053	0.319	0.119	0.495	0.027	0.200
Age	28.03	4.78	26.08	5.44	28.84	4.22
Years of Schooling	11.39	2.41	10.54	2.47	11.74	2.29
Higher Education	0.570	0.495	0.312	0.463	0.677	0.468
Married	0.274	0.446	0.181	0.385	0.312	0.463
Having children	0.329	0.470	0.210	0.407	0.378	0.485
Western or Danish	0.937	0.242	0.895	0.307	0.955	0.207
Sample Size	1,199,539		350,515		849,024	

Source: Own calculations on data from Statistics Denmark

Table 13: Heckman Two-step Estimation, 2nd Step, UI

Dependent Variable	No. of Arrests	
$[87-90] \times$ Farum	0.00152	(0.00108)
$[91-97] \times$ Farum	0.00022	(0.00074)
$[98-01] \times$ Farum	0.00062	(0.00088)
$[87-01] \times$ Farum	0.00082	(0.00072)
$[87-97] \times$ Farum	0.00049	(0.00068)

Note: Standard errors are in parentheses.
Sample size is 947,038.

Figure 7: Arrest Rate, UI Men, 1981-2005

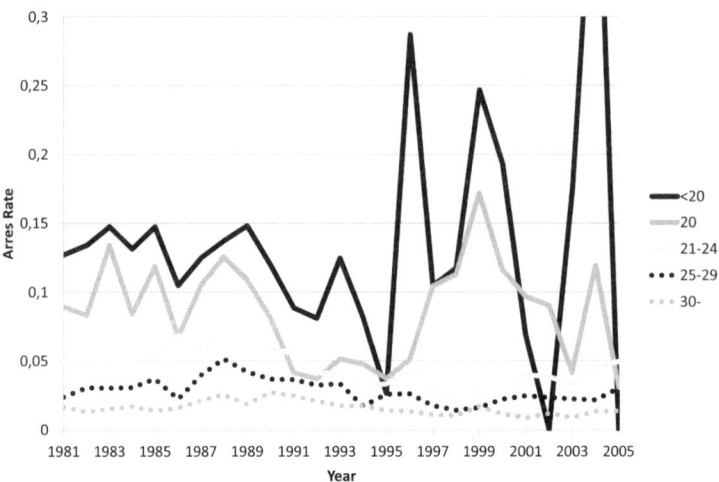

Source: Own calculations on data from Statistics Denmark

Figure 8: Income Sources, min. 75% Public Dependency, 1984-2005

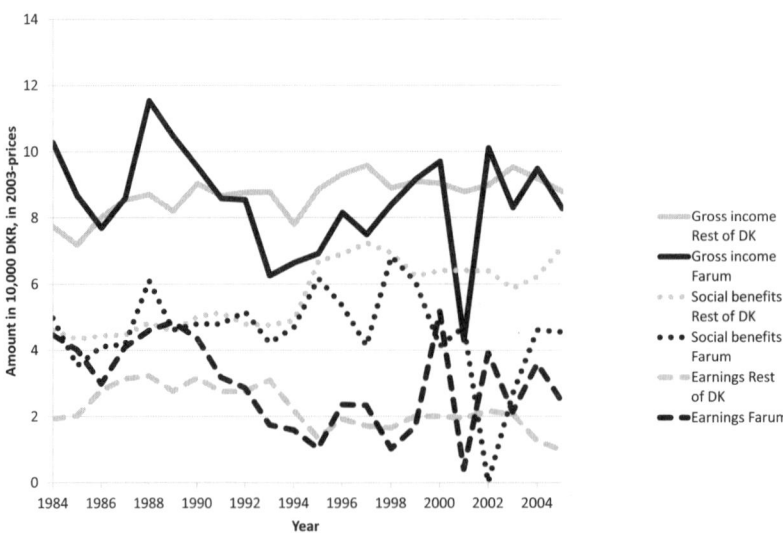

Source: Own calculations on data from Statistics Denmark